CROCHET HATS AND

MW00916709

Complete step by step guide to learn
how to crochet beautiful crochet Beanie
Hat patterns with several crochet
projects

Jenny Marvel

Table of contents

CHAPTER ONE

Introduction

Crochet hat styles demonstrate the ongoing appeal and utility of handcrafted apparel. Crocheted hats provide a distinct combination of warmth, style, and personality in a world dominated by mass-produced commodities. Whether you're a seasoned crafter or just starting out with crochet, the fascination of making something with your own hands goes beyond usefulness and becomes a form of self-expression.

Crochet hats become more than simply accessories as each stitch is meticulously constructed; they are expressions of individuality and creativity. In today's fast-paced world, when fashions change in the flash of an eye, a handcrafted hat has a soothing timeless quality. It speaks of heritage, workmanship, and the importance of devoting time to creating something worthwhile.

Furthermore, crochet hat designs suit a broad variety of interests and preferences. From traditional beanies that conjure nostalgia to fashionable slouchy hats that radiate casual elegance, there's a pattern for every aesthetic. Furthermore, crochet's versatility allows for limitless customization—from selecting the ideal yarn and color palette to adding decorations that suit your own style.

As we explore the universe of crochet hat designs, we will go on a voyage of creativity and self-discovery. Through the rhythmic motion of our hooks and the interplay of colors and textures, we bring simple strands of yarn to life, changing them into comfortable companions for life's experiences. So, let us explore the many possibilities that crochet has to offer, and experience the delight of creating everlasting masterpieces with our own two hands.

Popularity and versatility of crochet hat patterns

Crochet hat designs have remained popular throughout history, across generations and countries. Their popularity stems not only from their usefulness as headgear, but also from their variety and aesthetic value. Crochet hats come in a variety of styles to fit any taste or occasion, ranging from traditional patterns to modern trends.

One of the most important aspects contributing to the popularity of crochet hat designs is their accessibility. Crocheting, unlike other types of creating, takes little equipment and knowledge, making it an excellent pastime for both beginners and experienced crafters. Anyone, regardless of skill level, can make a gorgeous and useful hat with just a hook and some yarn.

Furthermore, crochet hat designs are very adaptable, allowing for limitless creativity and modification. Whether you favor basic, subtle patterns or vibrant, eye-catching ones, there is a crochet hat pattern to suit you. From delicate lacework to comforting cables, the options are literally endless.

Another reason crochet hat styles have remained popular is their practicality. Crochet hats are not only fashionable, but also utilitarian, offering warmth and protection from the weather. A crochet hat is both attractive and utilitarian, whether you're fighting the cold winter weather or protecting yourself from the sun's rays.

Crochet hat styles have also gained popularity in recent years, thanks to a renewed interest in handcrafted objects and traditional crafts. In a world dominated by mass-produced commodities, people are increasingly appreciating the craftsmanship and uniqueness of handcrafted objects. Crochet hats, with their distinct textures and handcrafted charm, provide a refreshing contrast to mass-produced fashion.

Crochet hat designs are popular because they are easy to make, versatile, utilitarian, and have an artisanal feel. Crochet hats are eternal emblems of creativity, self-expression, and tradition, as we continue to appreciate the beauty of handcrafted handicraft.

The importance of handcrafted things

In today's fast-paced world of rapid fashion and large manufacturing, handcrafted things are especially valuable. They convey a feeling of connection, authenticity, and workmanship in contrast to many contemporary commodities, which are impersonal and disposable.

When it comes to headgear, the value of handcrafted objects is very clear. Hats are more than simply functional accessories; they can represent personal style and individuality. A handcrafted hat retains the creator's care and attention, imbuing it with warmth and originality that factory-made alternatives cannot match.

Furthermore, handcrafted hats provide for a degree of customisation and individuality that mass-produced products cannot provide. Handmade hats allow for limitless creativity and self-expression, whether it's picking the ideal yarn, designing a one-of-a-kind stitch pattern, or adding customized decorations.

Beyond their visual appeal, handcrafted hats have emotional importance. They often become treasured keepsakes, handed down from generation to generation as physical mementos of love, creativity, and shared experiences.

In addition to their emotional value, handcrafted hats provide functional advantages. They are often made with higher-quality materials and more attention to detail than mass-produced competitors, resulting in enhanced longevity and comfort.

Overall, the significance of handmade objects in headgear stems not only from their visual appeal, but also from their capacity to link us to our creativity, history, and others. In an increasingly impersonal society, handcrafted hats serve as a pleasant reminder of the beauty and worth of handicraft.

A preview of the many hat designs to be explored

Crochet hat designs are as diverse as the creators' ideas. From timeless classics to cutting-edge trends, there is a hat design for every style, season, and event.

Classic beanies remain a perennial favorite, providing a classic and adaptable alternative for daily wear. Whether you like a basic ribbed design or a more intricate stitch pattern, there's a beanie pattern for you.

Slouchy hats are a wonderful alternative for individuals who want to wear something more relaxed and informal. These fashionable but simple designs exude a relaxed attitude that's ideal for weekends and leisurely adventures.

Seasonal favorites abound in the realm of crochet hat patterns, with designs to fit every temperature or occasion. Every season has its own hat design, from lightweight summer caps to snug winter beanies.

Trendy twists on classic patterns provide a new twist to classic styles, with vivid colors, whimsical decorations, and surprising features that are guaranteed to turn attention.

Crochet hat designs allow you to experiment with numerous styles and trends, as well as customize them. Whether you're a novice hoping to improve your abilities or an experienced crafter looking for a new challenge, there's always something new to learn and discover in the world of crochet hat designs. So take your hook and some yarn, and let your imagination go wild as you discover the limitless possibilities of crochet hat creation.

Tools and materials needed

Crocheting hats and beanies requires the proper supplies and equipment for a good effort. Here's a more detailed explanation of the supplies and tools you'll need:

Yarn:

Yarn is the primary material used to crochet hats and beanies. Select a yarn that is appropriate for the project based on criteria like as weight, fiber content, and color.

For hats and beanies, you'll want to pick a yarn that's soft, comfy to wear, and long lasting. Worsted weight (medium) and bulky weight (chunky) are popular yarn weights for hats, although finer yarns such as sport weight or DK weight may also be used for lighter hats.

Consider the yarn's fiber makeup, which might be acrylic, wool, cotton, or a combination. Each kind of yarn has distinct properties in terms of warmth, breathability, and maintenance needs. Choose yarn colors that will compliment the design of your cap or beanie. Solid colors, variegated yarns, and self-striping yarns may all provide unique visual effects.

Crochet hooks:

Crochet hooks are the principal equipment for creating stitches in crochet crafts. Choose a crochet hook size that matches the yarn weight you're using.

Most hat and beanie projects utilize hook sizes ranging from H/5mm to J/6mm, depending on the yarn weight and desired tension.

Crochet hooks come in a range of materials, such as metal, plastic, wood, and ergonomic designs. Choose a material and style that is comfortable in your hand and enables you to crochet for long periods of time without pain.

Stitch markers:

Stitch markers are handy for identifying certain stitches or rounds in your crochet work. They may help you keep track of stitch counts, pattern repetitions, and shaping aspects in your beanie or cap.

Stitch markers come in a variety of styles, including locking, split-ring, and detachable. Choose markers that may be easily inserted and removed as required during your job.

Yarn Needles:

A yarn needle, often called a tapestry needle or a darning needle, is used to weave yarn ends and stitch seams in crochet creations.

Choose a yarn needle with a big eye to handle the thickness of your yarn. Plastic or metal yarn needles are regularly used and available in a variety of sizes to accommodate different yarn weights.

Scissors:

A pair of sharp scissors is required for cutting yarn and clipping loose ends in crochet projects.

Choose scissors with a comfortable grip and a sharp tip for accurate cutting.

Keep these available when crocheting to cut yarn as required throughout your creation.

Blocking tools (optional):

Blocking mats, T-pins, and steam irons may be used to shape and smooth your completed beanie or cap.

Blocking may assist to increase stitch definition, balance out tension, and mold the finished object to the desired size. It is especially excellent for work involving lace or textured stitching.

Gathering these supplies and equipment before beginning your crochet project will ensure that you can easily and confidently construct stunning hats and beanies.

CHAPTER TWO

Classic Beanies

Classic beanies are timeless favorites in the field of crochet hat designs, providing a balance of simplicity, adaptability, and warmth. These snug-fitting hats are ideal for staying warm during cold weather while also adding a touch of flair to any outfit.

Classic beanies come in a variety of designs to choose from. From classic ribbed designs that inspire nostalgia to more contemporary adaptations with distinctive stitch patterns and decorations, there's a beanie pattern for everyone's taste and aptitude.

One of the distinguishing features of traditional beanies is their simplicity. Many designs use simple stitches like single crochet, double crochet, and half double crochet, making them suitable even for novices. Crafters may build attractive and useful hats for regular wear using just a few basic methods.

Furthermore, traditional beanie patterns typically allow for modification and personalization. Whether it's selecting the ideal yarn in your favorite color, adding a whimsical pom-pom or tassel, or playing with various stitch patterns, there are many ways to put your own stamp on a basic beanie design.

Classic beanies are valued for both their aesthetic appeal and their functionality. Their tight fit traps heat and keeps the head warm in chilly conditions, making them must-have winter wardrobe pieces. A classic beanie is a flexible and vital friend, whether you're hitting the slopes, battling the morning commute, or just taking a leisurely walk.

Overall, traditional beanies are the ideal combination of elegance and usefulness, providing timeless appeal that spans fads and seasons. Whether you're an experienced maker or just starting out, discovering the universe of traditional beanie designs is guaranteed to inspire and excite. So take your hook and some yarn, and set off on a quest to create timeless beanies.

Traditional ribbed beanie design

The traditional ribbed beanie design is a timeless classic that combines simplicity and beauty. Its defining characteristic is the ribbed texture, which is generated by alternating rows of knit and purl stitches, adding visual interest while also providing a tight and elastic fit.

To begin making a conventional ribbed beanie, choose your desired yarn and the suitable hook size depending on the yarn weight. Worsted weight yarn is widely used for beanies because it provides a blend of warmth and flexibility. Once your supplies are ready, you may begin by making a foundation chain of stitches, usually in multiples of two.

After finishing the foundation chain, you'll work in rows of ribbed stitches, alternating between knit and purl stitches to get the characteristic ribbed texture. The "2x2 rib," in which you knit two stitches and purl two stitches, is the most frequent ribbing design.

As you continue to knit the rows, the ribbed texture will gradually develop, resulting in an elastic and formfitting fabric. You may alter the length of the beanie to get the perfect fit, whether it's a tight skullcap or a somewhat slouchy style.

To complete the beanie, collect the stitches at the crown using a technique called "cinching" or "closing." Thread a yarn needle through the remaining stitches and pull tight to seal the top of the beanie. To finish, weave in any loose ends and add optional decorations like a pom-pom or decorative button to customize your creation.

Overall, the classic ribbed beanie design strikes an ideal balance of simplicity, elegance, and usefulness. Its classic style makes it a versatile addition to any wardrobe, and the elastic ribbed texture offers a comfortable and tight fit.

Simple single crochet beanie with optional pom-pom

The easy single crochet beanie is ideal for both beginners and experienced crocheters. Its simple structure and basic design make it an adaptable canvas for creativity, whether you want a clean and minimalist appearance or want to add whimsical elements like pom-poms or buttons.

To begin working on your easy single crochet beanie, first choose your yarn and hook size. Worsted weight yarn is a popular option for beanies because it provides a nice blend of warmth and flexibility, and using a hook size that matches the yarn weight ensures a tight and durable fabric.

Once your supplies are ready, you'll start by crocheting a foundation chain of stitches, then link the ends to make a ring. From there, work in continuous rounds of single crochet stitches, progressively increasing the number of stitches in each round to achieve a circular shape.

As you continue to crochet, the beanie will gradually take shape, with the single crochet stitches creating a thick and snug fabric that offers great warmth and insulation. You may change the height of the beanie to get the fit you want, whether it's a tight skullcap or a little slouchy profile.

Once you've reached your chosen length, secure the yarn and weave in any loose ends to complete the beanie. If you're feeling crafty, you can add a fun pom-pom to the beanie's crown using a pom-pom machine or by hand.

Overall, the easy single crochet beanie design provides an excellent balance of easiness and adaptability, making it a great project for crocheters of all skill levels. Whether you're making a simple beanie for regular use or adding fanciful embellishments for a pop of personality, this design will provide a fashionable and utilitarian item that will keep you warm and snug throughout the winter.

Instructions for adjusting size to fit all ages

One of the many benefits of crocheting hats is the flexibility to adjust the size to match any age or head size. Whether you're knitting a beanie for a newborn or a huge adult, there are easy strategies for adjusting the size and ensuring a great fit.

To begin, you need have a fundamental grasp of head circumference measures. Standard head circumference measurements for various age groups may be found online or measured directly with a soft measuring tape.

Once you've measured your head circumference, you may use it to change the amount of stitches in your foundation chain or beginning round. For example, if you're knitting a beanie for a newborn infant with a 14-inch head circumference, begin with a foundation chain or beginning circle that is about 12 inches long, allowing for some flexibility to guarantee a tight fit.

Similarly, if you're constructing a beanie for an adult with a 22-inch head circumference, alter the amount of stitches to produce a bigger first round. Keep in mind that the number of stitches required may vary according on the yarn weight and hook size used, so always prepare a gauge swatch and adjust appropriately.

In addition to modifying the beginning size, you may also change the length of the beanie to get the right fit. For example, you might build a shorter beanie for a tighter fit or a longer beanie for a slouchy appearance.

Overall, learning how to modify the size of your crochet hats allows you to make elegant and comfortable accessories for everybody in your life, from infants to adults. With a little forethought and imagination, you can make sure that your handcrafted hats are not only attractive but also completely fitted to the wearer's specific specifications.

CHAPTER THREE

Stylish Slouchies

Stylish slouchy hats are a modern take on the traditional beanie, with its relaxed and casual form providing an air of easy sophistication to any ensemble. These flexible accessories are ideal for adding individuality to your clothing while keeping you toasty and warm during colder months.

Creating a fashionable slouchy hat starts with choosing the appropriate yarn and hook size to get the correct drape and texture. Worsted weight or chunky yarns are often used for slouchy hats, since they give the essential bulk and structure to achieve the trademark slouchy style.

Once your supplies are ready, you'll begin by crocheting a foundation chain or beginning round, then work in continuous rounds of basic stitches like single crochet, double crochet, or half double crochet. Unlike regular beanies, slouchy hats are often longer in length and have looser tension, enabling the fabric to droop and drape naturally while worn.

As you continue to crochet, the hat will gradually take shape, with the slouchy silhouette appearing as you increase the amount of stitches in each round. Depending on your style, you may change the length of the hat to obtain the ideal amount of slouchiness, whether it's a subtle slouch or a more noticeable drape.

In addition to the basic slouchy hat design, there are other variants and decorations you may use to personalize your hat and make it really unique. To add texture and visual interest to your hat, try doing various stitch patterns like chevrons, cables, or lacework. To customize your creation and set it apart from the crowd, consider adding colorful decorations such as pom-poms, tassels, or buttons.

Overall, elegant slouchy hats are a fun and trendy accessory with limitless potential for creativity and customisation. Whether you're crocheting a hat for yourself or as a present for a friend, a trendy slouchy hat can add flare to any ensemble while keeping you looking smart and comfortable all season.

Introduction to slouchy hat style and its modern appeal

Slouchy hats, with their relaxed shape and informal mood, have evolved as a fundamental item in modern design, providing the ideal balance of comfort and style. Unlike typical beanies, which hug the head tightly, slouchy hats have a looser design, additional length, and fabric that provides a relaxed, "slouchy" appearance when worn.

One of the main draws of slouchy hats is their adaptability. A slouchy hat lends a touch of easy style to any ensemble, whether you're doing errands, seeing friends for coffee, or going on a weekend trip. It's the ideal accessory for days when you want to appear polished without exerting too much effort.

Furthermore, slouchy hats offer a contemporary charm that reflects current fashion trends. Their loose silhouette and informal appearance make them an ideal compliment to a variety of looks, from athleisure to boho chic. A slouchy hat instantly adds individuality and flare to any outfit, whether it's jeans and a t-shirt or a flowing maxi dress.

Slouchy hat designs are popular among crafters because to their attractive appeal, as well as their ease and adaptability. Crocheters may make a variety of slouchy hat styles using just a few basic stitches and some creative flair, ranging from simple solids to vibrant stripes and complex textures. It's a project that's as fun to create as it is to wear.

In addition to their fashionable appeal, slouchy hats have functional advantages. Their extended length and fabric give additional warmth and covering, making them great for staying comfortable during colder weather. Furthermore, their loose fit makes them comfy to wear all day, whether inside or outside.

Overall, slouchy hats have become a must-have item for anybody trying to inject a touch of contemporary refinement into their outfit. With its relaxed shape, informal atmosphere, and unlimited style options, it's no surprise that slouchy hats have become popular among fashionistas and makers alike.

Chevron stitch slouchy hat pattern

The chevron stitch slouchy hat design is a fashionable and eye-catching take on the traditional slouchy hat, with bright chevron stripes that give color and texture to any outfit. This design blends the classic charm of the slouchy form with the geometric beauty of the chevron stitch, creating a hat that is as enjoyable to wear as it is to knit.

To begin making your chevron stitch slouchy hat, first choose your yarn and hook size. Worsted weight yarn is ideal for this design because it offers the essential structure and drape to highlight the chevron stitch pattern, and a hook size that matches the yarn weight ensures a tight and comfortable fit.

Once you've prepared your supplies, begin by crocheting a foundation chain of stitches, then work in rounds of the chevron stitch design. The chevron stitch is made by alternating between single crochet, double crochet, and half double crochet stitches, with increases and reductions at key spots to form the characteristic V-shaped pattern.

As you continue to crochet, the chevron stripes will gradually appear, giving a visually appealing appearance that adds depth and character to the hat. Depending on your preferences, you may use a single color for a more subtle design or combine numerous colors to create dramatic and vivid stripes.

As you approach the desired length of the hat, finish with a round of single crochet stitches to make a neat and finished edge. Finally, secure the yarn and weave in any loose ends to finish your chevron stitch slouchy hat.

Overall, the chevron stitch slouchy hat design provides an excellent balance of style, comfort, and inventiveness. Whether you wear it on a cold day or to add a splash of color to your ensemble, this hat is guaranteed to turn attention and become a beloved addition in your closet.

Textured puff stitch slouchy hat design

The textured puff stitch slouchy hat pattern is an ideal combination of comfortable comfort and sophisticated design. This design makes use of the puff stitch, a raised stitch that gives the hat a distinctive texture suggestive of puffy clouds, adding visual interest as well as tactile appeal. Crafting this hat provides a completely immersive crocheted experience, with each puff stitch adding depth and character to the completed product.

To begin your crocheting adventure, collect the following materials: a suitable yarn, ideally in a medium weight for a balanced texture, and a crochet hook that matches to the yarn weight. Choose a color palette that reflects your own style, whether you like peaceful neutrals, lively colors, or a combination of the two.

Starting with a foundation chain, you'll create the base of your hat, making sure it's broad enough to comfortably wrap around the wearer's head. As you proceed, the puff stitch will become the star of the show. This stitch involves drawing up numerous loops in a single stitch, resulting in a small "puff" that gives depth and texture to the cloth.

As you go through each round, you'll see the hat's texture changing, with rows of puffs creating beautiful patterns that dance over the surface. The puff stitch's repetition not only makes an appealing texture, but it also adds a contemplative rhythm to the crocheting process, enabling you to immerse yourself in the flow of the stitches.

Once you've achieved the required length for your hat, you'll go on to the brim, where you may experiment with various edging methods to finish your masterpiece. Whether you choose a basic ribbed border or a beautiful scalloped edge, the finishing touches transform your hat from a useful item to wearing art.

Finally, the textured puff stitch slouchy hat is more than simply a piece of headgear; it's a labor of love that demonstrates your maker skills and originality. Whether you keep it for yourself or give it to a loved one, this hat will be adored for its beauty, warmth, and the many hours of artistry that went into its production.

Tips for creating the ideal slouch in your hats

Creating the ideal slouch in your hats is an art form that requires a careful balance of tension, length, and drape. Here are some pointers to help you master the art of creating slouchy hats:

1. Select the appropriate yarn: Choose a yarn with nice drape and elasticity, such a soft acrylic or a wool mix. Avoid using stiff or bulky yarns, since they may cause the hat to stand up too straight or lack the correct droop.

2. Experiment with hook size to get desired drape and slouchiness in your crochet hat. To make a looser garment with greater drape, use a bigger hook size than is advised for the yarn weight.

3. Consider hat length: The length of your hat determines the degree of slouch. Crochet the hat longer before

commencing the crown reductions to get a more dramatic droop.

4. To produce additional slouch, add extra rounds of stitches around the crown.

5. Check the fit: Try on the hat and tweak the length or tension to create the appropriate slouch.

6. Block your final hat to shape and define the slouch, particularly if using a yarn with considerable drape. Simply moisten the hat, mold it into the appropriate slouch, and let it dry flat.

By adding these guidelines into your crocheting technique, you'll be well on your way to making slouchy hats that are fashionable, comfy, and just right. With little trial and experience, you'll soon be able to get the right slouch in your hats.

CHAPTER FOUR

Tips and Techniques

To master crochet hat designs, you must pay close attention to detail and have a thorough understanding of numerous tips and methods. Here's a quick summary of some important strategies and approaches to improve your hat-making abilities:

1. Select the proper yarn for the season and desired texture. When choosing yarn for your project, consider aspects such as fiber composition, weight, and color.

2. Always produce a gauge swatch to verify your hat is the right size. Adjust your hook size as needed to meet the pattern's gauge.

3. Maintain continuous tension during crocheting for even stitches and professional-looking results.

4. Learn how to combine rounds flawlessly to minimize apparent seams or holes in your hats.

5. Understand crochet stitch anatomy, such as loops, posts, and increases/decreases, for precise pattern execution.

6. Consider blocking your final hat to enhance its form and fit. Blocking may also assist to level out any uneven stitches.

7. Customize patterns to your taste. Experiment with various stitch patterns, colors, and accessories to personalize each hat.

8. Finishing touches: To get a finished appearance, weave in ends neatly, add ornamental components (e.g. buttons or appliques), and block your hat.

By adding these ideas and methods into your crochet arsenal, you'll be ready to tackle any hat design with confidence and originality. Whether you're a novice or an expert crocheter, understanding these techniques will allow you to produce hats that are not only beautiful and comfortable, but also represent your workmanship and creative vision.

Advice on Choosing the Right Yarn for Your Project

1. Fiber content: Consider the yarn's fiber content and its impact on the hat's feel and functionality. Natural fibers such as wool, alpaca, and cotton

provide warmth, breathability, and durability, but synthetic fibers like as acrylic and polyester are often less expensive and easier to care for.

2. Select a yarn weight that matches the required thickness and warmth for your hat. Lighter weights, like as lace or fingering yarns, are appropriate for lightweight, breathable hats, but larger weights, such as worsted or bulky yarns, are best for thick, snug hats.

3. Seasonality: Consider the hat's intended wear season before picking yarn. For summer hats, use lightweight, breathable yarns like cotton or bamboo, while wool or acrylic yarns are warmer and more insulating.

4. Texture: Consider the yarn's texture and how it affects the look and feel of

the hat. Smooth yarns are great for displaying stitch patterns and generating crisp, clear lines, whilst textured or novelty yarns give visual interest and depth to your hat.

5. Color: Select yarn colors that match the wearer's style and desire. Solid colors are adaptable and timeless, although variegated or self-striping yarns may give depth and intricacy to your hat design.

6. Consider the cost of yarn when choosing supplies for a hat project. High-quality, premium yarns may be more costly, but they may improve the appearance and feel of your hat, whilst budget-friendly choices provide

affordability without compromising quality.

7. Consider yarn availability when purchasing extra skeins or matching colors for various projects. Choose yarns that are widely available and easily accessible at local yarn stores or internet merchants.

8. Check the yarn's wash and care instructions to verify it is appropriate for the intended application. Machine-washable yarns are ideal for daily use, however hand-wash or dry-clean only yarns may need additional care and upkeep.

By carefully examining these variables when choosing yarn for your hat project, you can guarantee that the completed hat is not only attractive and useful, but also properly tailored to the wearer's requirements and tastes.

Essential crochet stitches and abbreviations used in the patterns

1. Chain stitch (ch): The foundation of many crochet projects, the chain stitch is used to create a starting row or foundation chain.

2. Single crochet (sc): A basic crochet stitch worked into one loop of the previous row, creating a dense and sturdy fabric.

3. Half double crochet (hdc): Similar to single crochet but with an extra step, resulting in a slightly taller stitch with more drape.

4. Double crochet (dc): A taller crochet stitch worked into one loop of the previous row, creating a more open and airy fabric.

5. Treble crochet (tr): A tall crochet stitch worked into one loop of the previous row, creating a very open and lacy fabric.

6. Slip stitch (sl st): A simple stitch used to join rounds, create decorative edges, or move across the fabric without adding height.

7. Increase (inc): Adding extra stitches in a single stitch or space to increase the width or circumference of the fabric.

8. Decrease (dec): Combining multiple stitches into a single stitch or space to decrease the

width or circumference of the fabric.

9. Magic ring (MR) or magic loop: A technique for starting projects in the round, allowing for a seamless and adjustable beginning.

10.   Stitch marker (sm): A tool used to mark a specific stitch or position in the fabric, helpful for keeping track of pattern repeats or shaping instructions.

11.   Repeat (rep): Indicates a sequence of stitches or instructions to be repeated multiple times within a row or round.

12.   Yarn over (yo): Wrapping the yarn around the hook before

working a stitch, used to create height and texture in taller stitches like double crochet and treble crochet.

These essential crochet stitches and abbreviations form the building blocks of most crochet patterns, including hat patterns. By mastering these fundamental techniques, you'll be well-equipped to tackle a wide range of crochet projects and create beautiful hats with confidence and skill.

Finishing methods

1. After finishing your hat, tie any stray yarn ends to avoid unraveling. Using a yarn needle, gently thread the ends through the stitches on the wrong side of the cloth, being sure to conceal them discreetly.

2. Blocking is the act of shaping and smoothing your final hat to get a professional appearance. Depending on the yarn and fiber content, you may wet block (soak the hat in water, shape, and dry) or steam block (form the hat without soaking). Blocking may assist to smooth out stitches, clarify stitch patterns, and enhance the overall look of your hat.

3. Consider embellishing your hat with ornamental components like buttons, pearls, or embroidery for a more appealing look. To achieve a polished look, sew them firmly onto the hat using matching thread or yarn.

4. Edging: Adding a tidy edging around the brim or bottom edge of your hat may provide a polished appearance.

Edging options include basic single crochet or slip stitch, beautiful picot edging, and ribbed edging for increased flexibility and texture.

5. Consider hand-labeling your hat with your name or business logo for a professional look. Labels may be sewed onto the interior of the hat or applied with a fabric glue for a customized touch.

6. Quality control: Check your hat for loose stitches, unequal tension, and other defects. Making the required corrections or revisions will result in a high-quality end product.

By combining these finishing methods into your crochet hat projects, you may improve the overall appearance and quality of your work, producing hats that are polished, professional, and ready to wear.

Troubleshooting Common Issues

1. Gauge mismatch may cause a hat to be too big or too tiny. Always prepare a gauge swatch before starting your project, and modify your hook size as required to fit the pattern's gauge.

2. Inconsistent tension leads to uneven stitches and an untidy look. Practice keeping a consistent tension when crocheting, and consider using a different hook size or modifying your grip as required.

3. Adjust the length of your hat to get the appropriate slouch. Adding more rounds around the crown may exacerbate slouch, while reducing rounds can alleviate it.

4. Uneven edges: Improper round joining or varying tension might cause uneven edges in your item. To guarantee equal edges, attach rounds firmly and with continuous tension.

5. To avoid yarn splitting when crocheting, use a different hook size or fiber composition. Some yarns are more prone to splitting than others, so experiment with several alternatives to discover the one that best suits your project.

6. To reshape a flat or deformed hat, try blocking it. Wet or steam block your hat to remove any unevenness and help it to maintain its intended form.

7. If your hat lacks flexibility, try using a different yarn or adding ribbing to the brim to provide stretch. Alternatively,

blocking your hat might make it stretch and fit better.

By diagnosing these typical concerns and adopting suitable solutions, you may overcome the hurdles of crocheting hats and obtain professional-looking outcomes that you'll be happy to wear or give to others.

CHAPTER FIVE

Beginner Crochet Hat and Beanie Patterns

1. Basic Ribbed Beanie

Materials needed:

• Choose a color for your worsted weight yarn. • Use a crochet hook suited for the yarn weight (usually size H/5mm).

• Yarn needle • Scissors.

• Optional: stitch markers.

Instructions:

Step 1: Start by forming a slip knot and crocheting a foundation chain. The amount of chains determines your hat's circumference. For a typical adult-sized hat, begin with a chain of 70-80 stitches.

Step 2: Join the ends of the foundation chain to make a ring, taking care not to twist it. You may attach with a slip stitch to the first chain or use a magic ring method if you want.

Step 3: Work in rounds of single crochet stitches (sc) around the ring. If you want to indicate the start of the round, use a stitch marker in the first stitch. Continue to crochet in a spiral, without linking rounds.

Step 4: Crochet in continuous rounds of single crochet until the hat is the desired length, which is usually 7-9 inches for an adult-sized hat. Adjust the length as required to get a tight or slouchy fit.

Step 5: Begin the ribbing pattern by alternately working front post double crochet (fpdc) and rear post double crochet (bpdc) stitches. This provides the ribbed texture. Work fpdc around the next stitch's post, then bpdc around the stitch after that. Repeat the pattern around the whole hat.

Step 6: Continue alternating fpdc and bpdc stitches for many rounds, usually 2-3 inches, to form the ribbed band at the hat's bottom.

Step 7: Finish the hat by fastening off the yarn and weaving in any loose ends with a yarn needle. Block the hat if necessary to shape and smooth the stitches.

2. Easy Double Crochet Hat

Materials required:

- Worsted weight yarn (color of choice)
- Crochet hook suitable for yarn weight (usually size H/5mm).
- Yarn needle • Scissors.
- Optional: stitch markers.

Instructions:

Step 1: Start by forming a slip knot and crocheting a foundation chain. The amount of chains determines your hat's circumference. For a typical adult-sized hat, begin with a chain of 70-80 stitches.

Step 2: Join the ends of the foundation chain to make a ring, taking care not to twist it. You may attach with a slip stitch to the first chain or use a magic ring method if you want.

Step 3: Work in rounds of double crochet (dc) around the ring. If you want to indicate the start of the round, use a stitch marker in the first stitch. Continue to crochet in a spiral, without linking rounds.

Step 4: Crochet in continuous rounds of double crochet until the hat is the desired length, which is usually 7-9 inches for an adult-sized hat. Adjust the length as required to get a tight or slouchy fit.

Step 5: Finish the hat by securing the yarn and weaving in any loose ends with a yarn needle. Block the hat if necessary to shape and smooth the stitches.

These step-by-step instructions should help you complete the Basic Ribbed

Beanie and Easy Double Crochet Hat designs. Happy crocheting!

3. Chunky Single Crocheted Beanie

Materials needed:

• Choose your favorite chunky yarn color. • Use a crochet hook suited for the yarn weight (usually size K/6.5mm).

• Supplies: yarn needle, scissors, and optional stitch marker.

Instructions:

Step 1: Start by forming a slip knot and crocheting a foundation chain. The amount of chains determines your hat's circumference. For a typical adult-sized hat, begin with a chain of 40-50 stitches.

Step 2: Join the ends of the foundation chain to make a ring, taking care not to twist it. You may attach with a slip stitch to the first chain or use a magic ring method if you want.

Step 3: Work in rounds of single crochet stitches (sc) around the ring. If you want to indicate the start of the round, use a stitch marker in the first stitch. Continue to crochet in a spiral, without linking rounds.

Step 4: Crochet in continuous rounds of single crochet until the hat is the desired length, which is usually 7-9 inches for an adult-sized hat. Adjust the length as required to get a tight or slouchy fit.

Step 5: Finish the hat by securing the yarn and weaving in any loose ends with a yarn needle. Block the hat if necessary to shape and smooth the stitches.

4. Simple Slouchy Hat

Materials needed:

• Choose your preferred color for the worsted weight yarn.

• Use a crochet hook that is adequate for the yarn weight (usually size H/5mm).

• Yarn needle • Scissors.

• Optional: stitch markers.

Instructions:

Step 1: Start by forming a slip knot and crocheting a foundation chain. The amount of chains determines your hat's circumference. For a typical adult-sized hat, begin with a chain of 70-80 stitches.

Step 2: Join the ends of the foundation chain to make a ring, taking care not to twist it. You may attach with a slip stitch to the first chain or use a magic ring method if you want.

Step 3: Work in rounds of double crochet (dc) around the ring. If you want to indicate the start of the round, use a stitch marker in the first stitch.

Continue to crochet in a spiral, without linking rounds.

Step 4: Crochet in continuous double crochet rounds until the hat reaches the required length, which is usually 9-10 inches for an adult-sized hat. Adjust the length as required to get a slouchy fit.

Step 5: Finish the hat by securing the yarn and weaving in any loose ends with a yarn needle. Block the hat if necessary to shape and smooth the stitches.

These step-by-step tutorials will walk you through the process of crocheting Simple Slouchy Hat designs. Happy crocheting!

5. Granny Square Beanie

Materials required: • Worsted weight yarn in different colors • Crochet hook suitable for yarn weight (usually size H/5mm) • Yarn needle • Scissors

Instructions:

Step 1: Start by crocheting a typical granny square. Begin with a magic ring or chain 4, then slip stitch to make a ring. Next, work the following into the ring: (3 double crochets, chain 2) - repeat three times. To link the initial double crochet, use a slip stitch. This is the center of your granny square.

Step 2: Continue working the granny square pattern by chaining 3 (which counts as a double crochet), followed by 2 double crochets into the previous round's chain-2 gap. Chain one, then work three double crochets into the same chain-2 space. Repeat the pattern (3 double crochet, chain 1, 3 double crochet) in each chain-2 gap around. Join with a slip stitch to the top of the chain-3.

Step 3: Continue to work rounds of the granny square, increasing each round by 4 stitches (3 in each corner and 1 in each side space). Continue until your granny square is the right size for the crown of your beanie.

Step 4: Once your granny square reaches the appropriate size, secure the yarn and weave in any loose ends.

Step 5: Fold your granny square diagonally to make a triangle. Seam the two sides together, leaving a hole for the hat's brim. This will form the crown of the beanie.

Step 6: To make the brim, connect your yarn to the slot at the bottom of the crown. Then, evenly distribute single crochet stitches along the edge of the opening. Continue to crochet in rounds until the brim reaches the

required width. Fasten the yarn and
weave in any loose ends.

6. Striped Baby Beanie

Materials needed:

• Worsted weight yarn in several
colors.

• Use a crochet hook that is adequate for the yarn weight (usually size G/4mm).

• Yarn needle • Scissors.

Instructions:

Step 1: Start by crocheting a foundation chain. For a baby-sized beanie, begin with a chain of 30-40 stitches, depending on the desired circumference.

Step 2: Join the ends of the foundation chain to make a ring, taking care not to twist it. You may attach with a slip stitch to the first chain or use a magic ring method if you want.

Step 3: Work in rounds of single crochet stitches (sc) around the ring. If you want to indicate the start of the round, use a stitch marker in the first stitch. Continue to crochet in a spiral, without linking rounds.

Step 4: Crochet in continuous rounds of single crochet until the hat is the required length for a baby-sized beanie, which is usually 5-6 inches.

Step 5: To add stripes, alternate colors at the start of each round as desired. Simply link the new color with a slip stitch and continue crocheting in single crochet pattern. When you're ready to swap colors again, cut the yarn and weave the ends together.

Step 6: Finish the hat by securing the yarn and weaving in any loose ends with a yarn needle. You may choose add a pom-pom or other decorations to the top of the beanie.

CHAPTER SIX

Intermediate Crochet Hat and Beanie Patterns

1. Cable Knit Beanie

Materials needed:

• Worsted weight yarn • Crochet hook (size H/5mm) • Cable needle or extra hook.

• Yarn needle • Scissors.

Instructions:

Step 1: Start by forming a slip knot and crocheting a foundation chain. The amount of chains determines your hat's circumference. For a typical adult-sized hat, begin with a chain of 70-80 stitches.

Step 2: Join the ends of the foundation chain to make a ring, taking care not to twist it. You may attach with a slip stitch to the first chain or use a magic ring method if you want.

Step 3: Work rounds of half double crochet stitches (hdc) around the ring.

If you want to indicate the start of the round, use a stitch marker in the first stitch. Continue to crochet in a spiral, without linking rounds.

Step 4: Crochet in continuous rounds of half double crochet until the hat reaches the required length, which is usually 7-9 inches for an adult-size hat. Adjust the length as required to get a tight or slouchy fit.

Step 5: To make the cable design, use front post double crochet (fpdc) and rear post double crochet (bpdc) stitches. Follow the cable pattern instructions for your selected design. Use a cable needle or a spare hook to secure stitches to the front or back as required.

Step 6: Continue to work the cable pattern for numerous rounds until the required height is achieved. Maintain the stitch count and tension to ensure that the cable pattern remains constant.

Step 7: Finish the hat by fastening off the yarn and weaving in any loose ends with a yarn needle. Block the hat if necessary to shape and smooth the stitches.

2. Lace Slouchy Hat

Material Requirements:

• Worsted weight yarn • Crochet hook (size G/4mm) • Yarn needle • Scissors.

Instructions:

Step 1: Start by forming a slip knot and crocheting a foundation chain. The amount of chains determines your hat's circumference. For a typical adult-sized hat, begin with a chain of 70-80 stitches.

Step 2: Join the ends of the foundation chain to make a ring, taking care not to twist it. You may attach with a slip stitch to the first chain or use a magic ring method if you want.

Step 3: Work in rounds of double crochet (dc) around the ring. If you want to indicate the start of the round, use a stitch marker in the first stitch. Continue to crochet in a spiral, without linking rounds.

Step 4: Crochet in continuous double crochet rounds until the hat reaches the required length, which is usually 9-10 inches for an adult-sized hat. Adjust the length as required to get a slouchy fit.

Step 5: To make the lace design, follow the lace stitch instructions included with the pattern. To get a lacey look, work clusters of stitches, chains, and skipped stitches together.

Step 6: Continue to work the lace design for numerous rounds until the required height is achieved. Maintain the stitch count and tension to ensure the lace design remains constant.

Step 7: Finish the hat by fastening off the yarn and weaving in any loose ends with a yarn needle. Block the hat if necessary to shape and smooth the stitches.

These step-by-step instructions will walk you through crocheting the Cable-

Knit Beanie and Lace Slouchy Hat designs. Enjoy your crocheting!

3. Textured Puff Stitch Beanie

Materials required:

• Worsted weight yarn • Crochet hook suitable for yarn weight (usually size H/5mm).

• Yarn needle • Scissors.

Instructions:

Step 1: Start by forming a slip knot and crocheting a foundation chain. The amount of chains determines your hat's circumference. For a typical adult-sized hat, begin with a chain of 70-80 stitches.

Step 2: Join the ends of the foundation chain to make a ring, taking care not to twist it. You may attach with a slip stitch to the first chain or use a magic ring method if you want.

Step 3: Work in rounds of single crochet stitches (sc) around the ring. If you want to indicate the start of the round, use a stitch marker in the first stitch. Continue to crochet in a spiral, without linking rounds.

Step 4: Crochet in continuous rounds of single crochet until the hat is the desired length, which is usually 7-9 inches for an adult-sized hat. Adjust the length as required to get a tight or slouchy fit.

Step 5: To make the textured puff stitch, follow the puff stitch directions in the design. Typically, this entails bringing up many loops in a single stitch to form a "puff" and attaching them with a chain stitch.

Step 6: Repeat the textured puff stitch pattern for multiple rounds, alternating with rounds of single crochet to produce a textured look. Maintain the stitch count and tension to ensure that the design remains constant.

Step 7: Continue working in the pattern until the hat reaches the required height, which is usually 1-2 inches from the top of the head for a tight fit.

Step 8: Finish the hat by fastening off the yarn and weaving in any loose ends with a yarn needle. Block the hat if necessary to shape and smooth the stitches.

4. Fair Isle Beanie

Materials needed:

• Multicolored worsted weight yarn.

• Crochet hook (size H/5mm), yarn needle, and scissors.

Instructions:

Step 1: Start by forming a slip knot and crocheting a foundation chain. The amount of chains determines your hat's circumference. For a typical adult-sized hat, begin with a chain of 70-80 stitches.

Step 2: Join the ends of the foundation chain to make a ring, taking care not to twist it. You may attach with a slip stitch to the first chain or use a magic ring method if you want.

Step 3: Work in rounds of single crochet stitches (sc) around the ring. If you want to indicate the start of the round, use a stitch marker in the first stitch. Continue to crochet in a spiral, without linking rounds.

Step 4: Crochet in continuous rounds of single crochet until the hat is the desired length, which is usually 7-9 inches for an adult-sized hat. Adjust the length as required to get a tight or slouchy fit.

Step 5: To make the Fair Isle colorwork pattern, use the chart or written instructions included with the design. This usually entails carrying different colors of yarn across the row and swapping colors as specified in the design.

Step 6: Repeat the Fair Isle pattern for many rounds, taking care to maintain consistent tension and weaving in the yarn ends as you go.

Step 7: Continue working in the pattern until the hat reaches the required height, which is usually 1-2 inches from the top of the head for a tight fit.

Step 8: Finish the hat by fastening off the yarn and weaving in any loose ends with a yarn needle. Block the hat if necessary to shape and smooth the stitches.

These step-by-step tutorials will walk you through the process of crocheting the Textured Puff Stitch Beanie and Fair Isle Beanie. Enjoy your crocheting!

5. Bobble stitch Beanie

Materials needed:

• Worsted weight yarn • Crochet hook
(size H/5mm) • Yarn needle • Scissors.

Instructions:

Step 1: Start by forming a slip knot
and crocheting a foundation chain. The

amount of chains determines your hat's circumference. For a typical adult-sized hat, begin with a chain of 70-80 stitches.

Step 2: Join the ends of the foundation chain to make a ring, taking care not to twist it. You may attach with a slip stitch to the first chain or use a magic ring method if you want.

Step 3: Work rounds of half double crochet stitches (hdc) around the ring. If you want to indicate the start of the round, use a stitch marker in the first stitch. Continue to crochet in a spiral, without linking rounds.

Step 4: Crochet in continuous rounds of half double crochet until the hat reaches the required length, which is usually 7-9 inches for an adult-size hat.

Adjust the length as required to get a tight or slouchy fit.

Step 5: To make the bobble stitch design, follow the directions given in the pattern. To produce a bobble, numerous loops are often pulled up in a single thread and secured with a chain stitch.

Step 6: Repeat the bobble stitch pattern for numerous rounds, alternating with rounds of half double crochet to produce a textured look. Maintain the stitch count and tension to ensure that the design remains constant.

Step 7: Continue working in the pattern until the hat reaches the required height, which is usually 1-2 inches from the top of the head for a tight fit.

Step 8: Finish the hat by fastening off the yarn and weaving in any loose ends with a yarn needle. Block the hat if necessary to shape and smooth the stitches.

6. Basketweave Beanie

Materials needed: • Worsted weight yarn • Crochet hook (size H/5mm) • Yarn needle • Scissors.

Instructions:

Step 1: Start by forming a slip knot and crocheting a foundation chain. The amount of chains determines your hat's circumference. For a typical adult-sized hat, begin with a chain of 70-80 stitches.

Step 2: Join the ends of the foundation chain to make a ring, taking care not to twist it. You may attach with a slip stitch to the first chain or use a magic ring method if you want.

Step 3: Work rounds of half double crochet stitches (hdc) around the ring. If you want to indicate the start of the round, use a stitch marker in the first stitch. Continue to crochet in a spiral, without linking rounds.

Step 4: Crochet in continuous rounds of half double crochet until the hat reaches the required length, which is usually 7-9 inches for an adult-size hat. Adjust the length as required to get a .tight or slouchy fit.

Step 5: To make the basketweave design, follow the basketweave stitch instructions included in the template. To generate the woven texture, normally work front post double crochet (fpdc) and rear post double crochet (bpdc) stitches together.

Step 6: Repeat the basketweave pattern for numerous rounds, alternating between front and back post stitches to get the woven look. Maintain the stitch count and tension to ensure that the design remains constant.

Step 7: Continue working in the pattern until the hat reaches the required height, which is usually 1-2 inches from the top of the head for a tight fit.

Step 8: Finish the hat by fastening off the yarn and weaving in any loose ends with a yarn needle. Block the hat if necessary to shape and smooth the stitches.

These step-by-step instructions should help you complete the Bobble Stitch Beanie and Basketweave Beanie designs. Enjoy your crocheting!

Made in the USA
Monee, IL
01 December 2024

71703294R00056